The Prestige Series

Hants &

Mike Caldicott and
Phil Davies

Cover: Having successfully negotiated the arch at Fareham railway station on 26th September 1966, **1272** (**KEL 715**), a 1950 lowbridge KSW6B, heads for the town's bus station. All three operators who had to pass under this arch (Hants & Dorset, Provincial and Southdown) operated highbridge vehicles; from time to time the negotiations were not so successful. It must have been a relief to all three when the bridge was rebuilt three years later. *(Bob Rowe)*

Rear cover: Timetable from March 1937. A nice period piece, although the double-decker is unlike any real vehicle ever operated by Hants & Dorset. *(Bob Rowe Collection)*

Inside front cover: It is Silver Jubilee year and a naval review is taking place in the Solent. Once again, open-top buses return to a Hants & Dorset service running between Gosport and Lee-on-Solent. This time it is on the 93, rather than the 72 as it was 25 years earlier, and the open-topper is green rather than cream. **3483** (**OPN 802**) had been new to Brighton, Hove & District in 1959; it moved to Hants & Dorset in 1976 from Southdown which explains its green livery when the rest of the fleet was by then in NBC red. Normally it was to be found at Poole depot. Number **1025** (**JEL 424E**), a Duple-bodied Bristol RESH6G, is seen after repaint into National livery. *(Bob Rowe; Geoff Coxon)*

Inside rear cover: Fleet number **3096** (**AJA 146B**), an ex-North Western Alexander-bodied Leyland Leopard and Leyland National No. **3730** (**WFX 255S**) on far-flung duties, the Leopard at the Gallowgate, Newcastle, premises of United Automobile Services and the National working on hire to West Yorkshire in Scarborough bound for Leeds. Both had come north on Hants & Dorset troop services *(see page 59). (Both: Geoff Coxon)*

Title page: In the summer of 1960, despite the increase in car ownership, Hants and Dorset was still attempting to stimulate leisure traffic by means of seasonal Sunday-only services to Lee-on-Solent. For that year only, the 84 was introduced from West End, operated by Woolston depot. The other three seasonal services, Nos 74, 79A and 94, first ran in the late 1950s, but all were discontinued after the 1963 season. Just for a brief period, six buses from no fewer than three 'foreign' Hants & Dorset depots lay over on the bus park next to Lee Tower. *(Bob Rowe)*

Below: This 1951 scene at Southampton shows, from left to right, a remarkable quintet of Leylands: **901** (**TR 5296**), 1928 TD1 with 1943 ECW 53-seat body; **971** (**LJ 9402**), 1934 TD3 with Brush 52-seat body; **995** (**BEL 391**), 1935 TD4 with Brush 53-seat body; **902** (**RU 7686**), 1928 TD1 with 1943 Beadle 52-seat body and **700** (**LJ 516**), 1929 LT1 with 1947 Beadle 32-seat body. *(Solent Transport Trust)*

Leyland Titan No. **124** (**TR 5327**) of 1928. The open-top, open-staircase 51-seat bodywork was by Short Brothers of Rochester. *(Hants & Dorset)*

EDITORIAL INTRODUCTION

Hants & Dorset Motor Services, for a variety of reasons, was not one of those companies that much attracted the interest or skills of the renowned transport photographer G H F Atkins, whose work has provided the material for the majority of the Prestige series books published so far. Geoffrey took the merest handful of typically excellent pictures of the operator, and these are being held over for use in a forthcoming *Prestige Series* title that will concentrate on his work in the south of England.

In the meantime, we at Venture Publications were delighted when Mike Caldicott and Phil Davies offered a Hants & Dorset illustrated survey for the series. There have coincidentally been a number of enquiries about other operators ("Why don't you do a Prestige on ... ?"), and readers who have similar texts and collections of pictures in their possession are invited to contact the publishers with a view to repeating this exercise.

Living within the erstwhile Hants & Dorset operating area, the authors have been able to bring a perspective to the story that would not otherwise have been possible. As a Tilling associated company for much of its life, Hants & Dorset followed a not untypical path for such an organisation. Concentrating on Leyland deliveries before the Second World War, it subsequently achieved, briefly, an all Bristol fleet.

Hants & Dorset Motor Services was perhaps a rather grand name for the company formerly known as Bournemouth & District, but since at the time of its renaming, the services crossed from one county to the other at the appropriately named County Gates, it obviously made sense. Considerable expansion eastwards meant that only two depots were ever to be located in Dorset proper, although it was ironical that, as a result of Local Government reorganisation, in 1974 Bournemouth found itself in Dorset.

Within the NBC the Company perhaps did not fare as well as some other subsidiaries and its final dissection - quartering, some might say - was maybe more than the long-standing Hants & Dorset enthusiast could endure. Perhaps the final glory days of Hants & Dorset could be regarded as being over by 1972, when the last true Hants & Dorset vehicle was painted Tilling green. This livery itself was one of Hants & Dorset's enduring features, for the particular hue of green often varied from bus to bus, because of, it was said, the effect of prevailing winds carrying salt air off the sea, which ran along the whole of the southern boundary of the Company's operating area.

Thanks are due the authors for their efforts, and gratitude must also be extended to all those enthusiast/photographers whose work does so much to bring to life a survey in published form such as this. Thanks must also go to Mary and Dave Shaw for reading the proofs and to Bob Rowe for converting the whole into a more than presentable publication.

John Banks
Romiley, Cheshire
July 2005

HANTS & DORSET MOTOR SERVICES LIMITED

The Company was first registered in March 1916 as Bournemouth and District Motor Services Limited, with W W Graham as its first General Manager. The first stage-carriage services were those between County Gates and Sandbanks, which were acquired, together with De Dion Bouton and Milnes-Daimler vehicles, from E Poulain and Canford Cliffs Motor Omnibus Co. Ltd in 1918. Premises were purchased at Norwich Avenue in Bournemouth and this became the Company's Head Office for almost the next thirty years. Early in 1920, the Company moved into the Southampton area with a route to Winchester and on 27th July that year the name of the Company was changed to Hants & Dorset Motor Services Limited. During the same year the company came under the joint control of the Tilling and British Automobile Traction organisations.

Several operators and their vehicles were acquired during the 1920s, among which were Lymington & District Motor Services in 1921, H & F Tutt and H W Smith of Gosport in 1924, T S Phipps of Netley in 1926 and C A Croucher of Lyndhurst in 1928. In 1924 an important agreement between the Company and Elliott Brothers Ltd (Royal Blue) of Bournemouth was reached, in which Hants & Dorset promised not to operate any excursions or long distance coach

Above: The first of many Leyland vehicles purchased by Hants & Dorset (then known as Bournemouth & District) was this single-decker which was new in April 1919; No. **8**, (**FX 4519**) originally carried a charabanc body, but is seen here in the early 1920s as a 34-seat Dodson-bodied open-top double-decker.

Below: Number **50** (**EL 5554**), a Leyland G5 of 1920, also with a Dodson body, on the Bournemouth to Shaftesbury service. The uniform of the period, in particular the overcoats and knee-high boots, were no doubt appreciated by the crews in the unheated vehicles. *(Both: Hants & Dorset)*

services from Bournemouth and in exchange Elliott Brothers undertook not to operate any stage-carriage services in the Bournemouth area. A through service from Bournemouth to Swanage commenced in 1927 and this entailed the use of the ferry between Sandbanks and Shell Bay to carry the buses across the entrance to Poole Harbour. The first vehicles to work this service were Leyland PLSC Lions, built in 1926/7.

Another agreement, with Poole Corporation in 1928, allowed Hants & Dorset to operate bus services within the Borough of Poole, with Bournemouth Corporation continuing to provide tram services between the two boroughs via Upper Parkstone. Hants & Dorset took over the Lower Parkstone route in 1929 and replaced the trams with new Leyland TD1 motor buses with outside staircases but covered-top bodies. Also in 1929, the Company acquired the Sandbanks - Poole service from Miss L Foott and in 1930 Poole and District Motor Services was acquired as were the Poole - Bere Regis and Dorchester services of G Vacher.

Vehicle livery up to 1930 was dark green with cream roofs and the Hants & Dorset fleet name was applied in a distinctive 'arched' form on each side. From 1930, the shade of green became a little lighter and the upper-saloon window surrounds of double-deckers were painted cream - the roofs of the earliest closed-top double-deckers (1929-34) being painted dark sand or black until 1935 when this area also became cream. Bus stations were constructed in the larger towns such as Southampton, Fareham and Winchester as well as the famous two-level structure at Bournemouth, which was opened in 1931 and which was shared with the coaches of Elliott Brothers (Royal Blue). The 1930s were to see further operators and vehicles acquired and the increase in the variety of vehicles led to the adoption in 1930 of class letters alongside the fleet numbers in order to distinguish the various types, thus:

A	Leyland GH7 of 1926/7
B	Leyland PLSC Lions of 1926-9
BB	Leyland LT1 Lions of 1929/30
C	Leyland PLSP2 Leviathans of 1927
D	Leyland Leverets of 1926/7
E	Leyland TD1 Titans of 1928-31
F	Leyland TS2, TS7 and TS8 Tiger

	saloons and coaches of 1929 and 1935-8
G	Leyland TD2 Titan of 1932
BG	Leyland LT5 Lions of 1932
H	Chevrolets acquired during 1930-3
J	Fords acquired in 1932/3
K	Guy OND saloons acquired in 1930
L	Leyland Cub saloons and coaches of 1933/6/9
M	Leyland TD2 of 1933
N	Daimler CF6 and ADC 424 acquired in 1935
P	Leyland TD4c of 1935 (later reclassified 'A' on removal of gearless transmission)
Q	AEC Q coaches acquired in 1935
R	Albion coach acquired in 1935 (reclassified S in 1936)
S	Issued to sundry acquired vehicles of 1935 and 1947
TD	Bristol K of 1938-49
TS	Bristol L saloons of 1938-48
TC	Bristol L coaches of 1947-9
A	Reissued to Leyland TD3 Titans of 1934 and Leyland TD4 Titans of 1935-7
BA	Leyland LT5A Lions of 1935
CD	Guy Arabs of 1943
J	Reissued to AEC Regal coaches acquired in 1935
K	Reissued to Dennis Ace saloons of 1934 and 1937
PD	Leyland PD1A of 1947/8

A variety of bodybuilders was employed during the 1920s including Kiddle, Dodson, Beadle, Brush, Leyland, Tilling and Short Brothers - the last named building the open-top bodies on the Leyland TD1s of 1928; Leyland bodywork was featured on the Leyland TD1 closed-top lowbridge double-deckers and Leyland LT1 saloons of 1929-31. Bodywork manufactured by Brush Electrical Engineering of Loughborough became the standard for double-deckers and saloons between 1932 and 1938, including the 20-seat Leyland Cubs, the large batch of Leyland TD3c and TD4c 'gearless' double-deckers of 1935 (purchased to replace the Bournemouth Corporation trams on the services between Bournemouth and Poole via Upper Parkstone) as well as the first batch of Bristol

Above: A view of the body shops at Southampton thought to have been taken during the conversion from solid to pneumatic tyres circa 1927. The body on the left is from a 1925 Leyland SG9, and that on the right is from a Leyland N type of 1923.

Below: This view clearly shows the arched style of fleet name adopted by the company in 1916 and used up to 1949. Fleet number **E82** (**TR 5296**) was a 1928 Leyland TD1, seen here at Southampton after having been fitted with a 1943 Eastern Coach Works 53-seat body. *(Both: Hants & Dorset)*

chassis in the fleet - K5Gs of 1938. Beadle bodywork was featured for the Leyland TS7 and TS8 coaches of 1935-8 and also for the Bristol L5G saloons purchased between 1938/40. The first examples of Eastern Coach Works (ECW) bodywork in the fleet were delivered in 1939 and 1940 on Bristol K5G chassis. Most of the Brush-bodied Leyland LT5A saloons of 1935 and many of the Beadle-bodied Bristol L5Gs of 1938-40 subsequently had a large area of the panelling in the rear overhang cut away in order to improve clearance on approaching and leaving the Sandbanks - Shell Bay ferry, which gave these vehicles a distinctive appearance.

Hants & Dorset acquired the tours and excursions, together with a number of coaches, from both Elliott Brothers (Royal Blue) of Bournemouth and Tourist Motor Coaches of Southampton in 1935. The coaches acquired from Royal Blue included Daimler CF6s and AEC Regals with Duple bodies; while those acquired from Tourist were Leyland TS2s with Strachan bodywork. Although Hants & Dorset acquired only a proportion of the business and vehicles from these two operators (the express services and around two thirds of the fleet passed to Western and Southern National), they were equally entitled to use the Elliott Brothers Royal Blue livery and fleet name and the two tone blue livery and fleet name of Tourist. The former was retained on all the coaches acquired from Elliott Brothers as well as being applied to new coaches bought in 1935/6; while the latter was retained on the vehicles acquired from Tourist Motor Coaches. However, in 1937 Hants & Dorset adopted a livery of green and cream, applied in an unusual manner and including the 'Hants & Dorset' fleet name, for its coaches. Most of the vehicles acquired from Elliott Brothers and Tourist were rebodied in 1937 with Beadle 28-seat front-entrance bodies. Included in the tours and excursions acquired were extended holiday tours to all parts of Great Britain from Lands End to John O' Groats. These tours were perpetuated right up to the formation of the National Bus Company and varied between 3 to 16 days. Coaches with a lower seating capacity than normal were used, so as to provide more legroom.

During the Second World War the Company lent a number of Leyland TD1 double-deckers to London Transport, but new Bristol and Guy chassis were delivered with Strachan and Roe utility bodies; from 1946 onwards the Company standardised on Bristol chassis with ECW bodies, at which time a revised livery of Tilling green with two cream bands together with Tilling-style underlined fleet name was introduced. This change occurred as a result of the 1942 split in the Tilling and BAT interests, when the company came under the control of the former. However, there were exceptions to this vehicle policy, such as the delivery of some all-Leyland PD2s and some AEC Regents with Northern Counties bodies in the late 1940s, as well as Beadle-, Dutfield- and Portsmouth Aviation-bodied Bristol coaches from 1947 to 1950. There were also a few Bedford OB saloons and coaches with Beadle and Duple bodies in 1949/50. Along with other companies within the Tilling group, Hants & Dorset was sold to the British Transport Commission with effect from 1st January 1948, but it retained its separate identity. On 1st January 1950, the fleet was completely renumbered, dispensing with the class letters used since 1930. Separate blocks of numbers were allocated as follows:

500 - 549	Service vehicles
550 - 568	Normal control 20-seat saloons
600 - 699	Coaches
700 - 846	Saloons
850 - 899	Coaches (from 1953)
900 - 1577	Double-deckers
2000 - 2076	Service vehicles (from 1953)
900 - 934	Coaches (from 1966)
3001 - 3057	Saloons (from 1968)

The fleet numbers were applied to the vehicles by means of pressed plates front and rear instead of transfers as used hitherto. From 1956, these plates were colour coded in order to denote depot allocations as follows:

Depot	Numerals	Background
Bournemouth	Black	White
Eastleigh	Black	Grey
Fareham	Black	Green
Lymington	Black	Orange
Parkstone	White	Black
Poole	Black	Blue
Ringwood	Black	Pink
Southampton	Black	Yellow

Above: Number **501** (**TK 1852**) in the postwar service fleet was a 1929 Leyland TD1, which was converted to a recovery vehicle in 1944; a Gardner 5LW oil engine replaced the Leyland petrol unit in 1952. The cab structure is all that remained of the original Beadle highbridge outside-staircase body as seen in this 1952 photograph at Bournemouth. *(Solent Transport Trust)*

Below: The first double-deckers in the fleet with enclosed staircases were lowbridge Leyland-bodied Leyland TD1s of 1930, exemplified by London-registered example **E138** (**UW 6977**) seen at Eastleigh in the 1930s. The London registration may have occurred as the vehicle was on loan to Tilling in London when new. Note the unusual destination linens with black lettering on a white background and also the rustic timber waiting room on the left. These were a feature of Hants & Dorset's operating area and were supplied by Twinn Brothers of Pokesdown. *(The Omnibus Society)*

| Winchester | White | Blue |
| Woolston | Yellow | Black |

Notable was the extensive rebodying and rebuilding activity, particularly during the 1950s and 1960s, in which Hants & Dorset undertook ambitious rebuilding of bodies to prolong their lives and to convert elderly coaches for stage-carriage work. Prior to the main body rebuilding programme, a large number of elderly Leyland TD2s of 1933 and Bristol K5Gs of 1938 were rebodied with new ECW lowbridge bodies in 1949. Some 1938-40 Bristol L5Gs also received new ECW 35-seat rear-entrance bodies at this time. Hants & Dorset's first major body rebuilding was of the Brush lowbridge bodies of two 1934/5 Leyland TD3s - 979/82 (OW 4245, ALJ 779) and four similarly bodied Bristol K5Gs of 1938 - 1015/7/24/30 (BTR 305/7, JT 9352/8). This work, in 1949-51, involved mounting all the windows in rubber flush with the exterior panels, replacing the original half-drop windows with sliding vents and fitting the then current three-aperture indicator display front and rear. The front of the bodies was made much more perpendicular in the process and the Bristol K5Gs received low radiators and deep-cab windscreens at this time. Similar but not quite so extensive rebuilding was then carried out on a number of 1939/40 Bristol K5Gs with ECW lowbridge bodies in 1952. Here the rebuilding was mainly confined to the front of the body and the fitting of low radiators and deep cab-windscreens. Then in 1952/3 Hants & Dorset constructed some open-top bodies in their own bodyworks at Southampton. Those built in 1952 were of six-bay construction and were mounted on wartime Bristol K5G and K6A chassis - 1106-11 (FRU 303-8). The first was fitted to a Leyland TD4 chassis of 1937 - 1005 (CRU 701) - but this body was transferred a year later to 1945 Bristol K6A No. 1112 (FRU 309). These open-top bodies were painted cream and had full-width fronts with concealed radiators and were a familiar sight in the summer season on the Bournemouth to Sandbanks routes for the next 16 years. Those built in 1953 were of similar general appearance but were of five-bay construction and were mounted on 1938 Bristol K5G chassis - 1011/2/9/20/5 (BTR 301/2/9/20, JT 9353). These bodies were subsequently transferred to 1947/8 Bristol K5G chassis -

1121/6/8/37/43 (GLJ 964/9/71/80/6) in time for the 1958 season.

In 1954, Hants & Dorset had ten prewar Bristol K5G chassis rebodied with new 8ft-wide ECW four-bay KSW-style highbridge bodies; 1013/24/30/1/3 (BTR 303, JT 9352/8/9/61) of 1938 and 1034/5/51/83/6 (ERU 262, 586, 602, FLJ 535/8) of 1939/40. Of these, 1013/34/5/51/83/6 were convertible to open-top and were painted in cream livery. This rebodying released the original ECW 53-seat bodies from 1034/5/51/83/6 for rebuilding by the Company and transfer to other 1939/40 Bristol K5G chassis. This set up a chain reaction and further ECW bodies from the ERU-, AFX-, APR- and FLJ registered K5Gs of 1939/40 were rebuilt and transferred to other chassis in the same group. This body rebuilding and body swapping commenced in late 1953 and continued into early 1956. Those rebuilt from 1954 onwards were given the full treatment of rubber-mounted windows, sliding side vents, upper-saloon front window vents and new indicators; but all these vehicles retained their original high radiators, albeit with slightly modified cab windscreens. In all, no fewer than eighteen 1939/40 ECW lowbridge bodies were rebuilt in this way - two examples being fitted to low-radiatored postwar chassis: body ex-1069 (APR 424) to 1950 Bristol K6B 1265 (KEL 708) in 1955 and body ex-1077 (APR 432) to 1946 Bristol K5G 1116 (FRU 827) in 1956. The latter remained in the fleet until 1972, having been converted for driver training in 1964; the body thus survived for no fewer than 32 years with Hants & Dorset.

Hants & Dorset's routes were mainly of a rural nature apart from local services in the Poole, Southampton and Fareham areas, which is why the Company standardised on the lowbridge design of double-decker, with its sunken side gangway in the upper saloon, prior to the appearance of the Bristol/ECW Lodekka. However, the first closed-top double-deckers in the fleet - twelve Leyland TD1s of 1929 (TK 1851-6, TR 6211-6), six with Beadle and six with Short Brothers bodies - were all of highbridge design with central gangway in the upper saloon. These vehicles, together with 15 Leyland lowbridge-bodied Leyland TD1s delivered later in the same year, were the last outside staircase double-deckers delivered new to the Company. The next highbridge double-

Above: Bus stations were constructed at various places during the 1930s, including Fareham, Southampton and Winchester, of which the latter is seen here. *(Hants & Dorset)*

Below: The famous two-level structure at Bournemouth was built in 1931 and is seen here some twenty years later with a Bristol KSW with Eastern Coach Works highbridge body descending the ramp from the upper level on a service to Poole. *(Solent Transport Trust)*

deckers in the fleet were delivered some 20 years later in 1949. These were six 56-seat Leyland-bodied Leyland Titan PD2/1s (JEL 496-501) which were a diverted South African export order. They spent their entire lives at Southampton depot and were a familiar sight on the services to the Fawley area for over ten years. Between November 1951 and May 1953, no fewer than 38 Bristol KSW6Bs and KSW6Gs were delivered with ECW 60-seat highbridge bodies: 1299-336 (KRU 965-87, LRU 51-65). The majority of these were allocated to Poole and Upper Parkstone depots for local town services; some of the later KSW6Gs were allocated to Southampton, Fareham and Winchester depots. Hants & Dorset received one of the six pre-production series Bristol/ECW Lodekkas in 1953, (1337 - LRU 67) and double-deck orders for the next 14 years were based on this design which enabled a central gangway to be placed in the upper saloon and yet remain within lowbridge overall height. However, it was not until 20 years later, in 1973, that the last side-gangway lowbridge double-deckers were withdrawn from the fleet. In 1957 the Company was allocated one of the six experimental 70-seat 30ft-long Bristol/ECW LDL6G Lodekkas, with a capacity of 70-seats (1406 - UEL 727). This originally had an open rear platform in line with the 19 shorter LD6Gs ordered at the same time. Further 30ft-long rear-entrance 70-seat Lodekkas were delivered in 1961/2. These were six FL6Bs, 1465-70 (4388-93 LJ) and six FL6Gs, 1482-7 (7682-7 LJ), which featured a flat lower-saloon floor and rear air suspension, these features being shared with the shorter 60-seat FS Lodekkas in the fleet. The FLs and many of the FSs also had driver-controlled doors for the rear platform. The forward-entrance FLF Lodekka entered the Hants & Dorset fleet in early 1965. The last examples, 1556-77 (KRU 223-7/35-41F, LEL 652-7F and LLJ 440-3F) delivered in 1967, were unusual in that they were fitted with semi-automatic transmission. Numbers 1562-7/73-7 were additionally unusual in that they had Leyland O.600 engines, the remainder having Bristol BVW units.

The first coaches in the fleet with Eastern Coach Works bodies were eleven Bristol LL6Bs and LWL6Bs delivered in 1951: 688-98 (KEL 731-6, KRU 995-9). All the bodies were 8ft-wide, fully fronted and had concealed radiators and were known as 'Queen Marys'. They introduced a new coach livery of cream relieved only by light green wings and wheels. The existing coach fleet was repainted from the earlier, more elaborate green and cream livery (introduced in 1937) into the new livery in time for the 1952 coaching season. The underfloor-engined Bristol/ECW LS6G coach made its appearance in the Hants & Dorset fleet in 1953 with the arrival of 699, 850-3 (MLJ 144-8). The bodies had 28 reclining seats and these coaches were used on extended holiday tours until 1960. Further ECW-bodied coaches based on the Bristol LS6G and MW6G chassis were delivered between 1956 and 1966. Examples from most batches did their turn on holiday tours, during which time their 39 fixed seats were exchanged for 30 recliners. Two examples of the 36ft-long Bristol RELH6G chassis with ECW 47-seat bodies were purchased in 1964: 898/9 (AEL 6/7B). In 1967-9 Bristol RESH and RELH chassis with Duple Commander bodies were ordered, thus ending a 16-year reign of ECW-bodied coaches in the fleet.

In 1956, Hants & Dorset commenced a programme of converting elderly coaches into one-man operated stage-carriage vehicles, a programme which continued in one form or another for almost the next 20 years. The first example was a 1948 Bristol L6B, 651 (HRU 364), the Beadle body of which retained its half-cab structure. A bay window was constructed across the bonnet between the cab and bulkhead to house the ticket-issuing machine. Subsequent conversions of the Beadle-, Dutfield- and Portsmouth Aviation-bodied Bristol L coaches involved the fitting of a full-width cab thus drastically altering the appearance of the vehicles, but the exposed radiators were retained. Between 1960 and 1962 no fewer than 18 Portsmouth Aviation-bodied Bristol L6A and L6G coach chassis were lengthened to 30 feet and were rebodied with new ECW 39-seat saloon bodies with full-width fronts. In general appearance they resembled the bodies to be found on Bristol SC chassis, but they had a different grille. The vehicles concerned were 663-6 (JRU 66-9) - LL6A (ex L6A); 670/1 (KEL 65/6) - LL5G (ex L6G) and 672-83 (KEL 67, 401-11) - LL6B (ex L6G). The Bristol AVW engines fitted to 672-83 were transferred from RLJ- and SRU-registered Bristol LD6B

Above: Leyland Titan **E234** (**TR 5055**), a 1929 Short Brothers-bodied open-topper, was converted for use as a tree-lopper. It is illustrated with its original body but in 1950 was rebodied for its treecutting duties and renumbered 500. *(John Banks Collection)*

Below: An all-Leyland line-up inside Fareham depot not long after the introduction of class letters to the fleet. On the right is a GH7; two PLSC1 Lions sandwich a closed-top Titan TD1. *(Bob Rowe Collection)*

Lodekkas of 1956/7 in exchange for the Gardner 6LW units from 672-83. Most of these ECW saloon bodies subsequently had their rear panelling cut away for use on the Sandbanks - Shell Bay ferry and as such these vehicles were a familiar sight on the Bournemouth to Swanage service in 1962-9. As far as the saloon fleet was concerned, the first underfloor LS entered service in 1953. Initially, these were fitted with two-door bodies, but the rear doorway was later removed. The first saloons to enter the fleet in the postwar period and to be used for one-man operation from new were a batch of Bristol MW5Gs, which entered service at Fareham depot in January 1959 (809-11, XEL 551-3). The next coaches to be converted for stage-carriage work, during 1963/4, were the ECW Queen Mary-bodied Bristol LL6Bs and LWL6Bs of 1951. Their fully fronted bodies required less conversion work than did the earlier half-cab designs and the alterations were virtually confined to opening up the bulkhead behind the cab, converting the sliding entrance door to power operation and fitting the then current style of route indicator in the front dome. Thirty-nine bus-type seats were fitted to all these vehicles, but 689-91/3 (KEL 732-4/6) each retained their original 35 coach seats at first.

The underfloor-engined Bristol LS6G and MW6G coaches were the next in line for stage carriage conversion and these required considerably less rebuilding than previous types. The work on the earlier conversions, affecting mainly the MLJ- and some of the SRU-registered batches of LS coaches, was a joint effort among ECW, Strachan of Hamble and Hants & Dorset during 1965/6. In these vehicles, jack-knife doors replaced the original outward- or inward-opening units and the coach seats were retained. The rest of the SRU- and all the UEL-registered LS6Gs, plus all but one of the YEL-registered MW6Gs were dealt with by Hants & Dorset during 1967 and their inward-opening doors were retained and converted to power operation. From 1960 to 1966, all the ECW-bodied Bristol MW6G coaches were delivered new to the Company with jack-knife entrance doors in readiness for future conversion for stage-carriage use. This work was undertaken by Hants & Dorset between 1968 and 1973 on the 1960-3 examples: 871-5 (6226-30 EL), 876-81 (1468-73 LJ), 882-7

(7118-23 LJ) and 888-90 (2688-90 RU) - 889/90 being conspicuous in retaining cream coach livery for a while. Bus-type seating replaced the coach seats in some of these conversions. Numbers 889/90 (2689/90 RU) - renumbered 1003/4 in 1971 - were repainted in red bus livery and fitted with 41 bus seats by ECW in 1974. Also in 1974, 1005/6 (2691/2 RU) were converted to stage carriage operation by ECW; but the coach seats were retained and red/white dual purpose livery was applied. Meanwhile in 1968, Hants & Dorset converted the four 1953 Bristol/ECW LS6B coaches acquired from Southern Vectis earlier in 1968 for stage-carriage work.

Hants & Dorset launched the first of its Limited Stop services in 1965: Bournemouth to Southampton via Ringwood and Cadnam which was numbered X27. This service was originally operated by a pair of Bristol FS Lodekkas painted in cream livery - 1511/2 (BRU 141B; CEL 860C) - but these gave way to 36ft-long saloons in 1969. Further Limited Stop services were subsequently introduced between Southampton, Fareham and Southsea (X71), Southampton and Gosport (X70), Southampton and Andover (X68), Bournemouth and Shaftesbury (X24) and Bournemouth and Salisbury (X38). Hants & Dorset's then General Manager, D W Morison, became additionally the General Manager of the neighbouring Wilts & Dorset Company in 1964. From January 1969, when the National Bus Company was formed to take over the fleets of the former Transport Holding Company and British Electric Traction group, Wilts & Dorset became legally owned by Hants & Dorset, but the only evidence of this was the appearance of the Hants & Dorset Motor Services Ltd name on the legal ownership panel of Wilts & Dorset vehicles and the registration of new Wilts & Dorset vehicles in Bournemouth instead of Wiltshire. Meanwhile, in 1966, the coach operations of Shamrock and Rambler and Charlies Cars of Bournemouth became part of the Transport Holding Company and this led, in May 1969, to Hants & Dorset acquiring the Southampton area operations of Shamrock and Rambler together with the following coaches:

| 926-8 | 604-6 LJ | AEC Reliance |
| | Duple C37F | New 1961 |

Many Brush- or Eastern Coach Works-bodied Leyland TD2s were delivered in 1932 and 1933. Most of them were rebodied between 1943 and 1949 by Beadle and Eastern Coach Works. Number **956** (**TK 8912**) was a 1933 example with a Beadle 52-seat body. *(Solent Transport Trust)*

929-31	525/9/32 CER	Bedford SB5	
	Duple C41F	New 1963	
932	FRU 420D	Bedford VAL14	
	Duple C52F	New 1966	
933	JEL 580E	Bedford VAL14	
	Duple C52F	New 1967	

The Shamrock and Rambler fleet name and livery of orange and cream were retained, but the Southampton operations of Shamrock and Rambler ceased in 1973, whereupon the vehicles were transferred to Shamrock and Rambler at Bournemouth.

Stage-carriage vehicle policy from the late 1960s favoured single- rather than double-deckers and large numbers of Bristol LHs and RELLs were delivered, the latter being superseded by Leyland Nationals from 1973. A number of the Bristol RELLs and Leyland Nationals had semi-coach seats for use on the Limited Stop services. However in 1971, six new Roe-bodied Daimler Fleetlines were diverted from the Gosport and Fareham Omnibus Company in exchange for six new Bristol RELLs. The Fleetlines had highbridge bodies (about 14ft 6ins tall) and four were allocated to Poole and two to Southampton depots originally. All six were subsequently based in the Poole area, though two were garaged at Swanage for a schools contract. The rear-engined Bristol VRT double-decker made its appearance in the fleet in late 1972 and there were eventually 150 vehicles of this type in service with the Company including six, with coach seats and painted in dual-purpose red and white livery, which entered service in 1976 on the Limited Stop routes from Southampton to Southsea and Gosport; and six from Southern Vectis which were acquired in 1979 in exchange for six convertible open-top VRTs - the latter had been delivered in late 1977, but because of service changes in the Bournemouth area in early 1978, the open-top summer-only route to Sandbanks passed to Bournemouth Corporation Transport and these VRTs never saw service in open-top form with Hants & Dorset. From 1970, new coaches in the fleet were Leyland Leopards with Plaxton bodies - the first Leyland coaches since the TS8 Tigers of 1938 and the first examples of Plaxton bodywork.

The fleet was again fully renumbered from 5th September 1971 using separate blocks of one hundred numbers above 1000 for the various vehicle types as follows:

1001 - 1027	Coaches, 10 metres long
1041 - 1044	Coaches, 10 metres long (Shamrock & Rambler, Southampton)
1051 - 1062	Coaches, 11 metres long
1091 - 1096	Coaches, 11 metres long (Shamrock & Rambler, Southampton)
1101 - 1168	Bristol FS Lodekka
1201 - 1212	Bristol FL Lodekka
1213 - 1274	Bristol FLF Lodekka
1299	Bristol LDL Lodekka
1338 - 1399	Bristol KS and KSW
1401 - 1498	Bristol LD Lodekka
1501 - 1515	Bedford VAM saloon
1521 - 1548	Bristol LH saloon
1603 - 1663	Bristol RELL saloon
1683 - 1699	Leyland Panther saloons ex-Maidstone & District
1761 - 1799	Bristol LS saloon (including former coaches)
1801 - 1860	Bristol MW saloon (including former coaches)
1901 - 1906	Daimler Fleetlines
9001 upwards	Service vehicles

The Wilts & Dorset fleet was similarly renumbered below 1000 at the same time. Self adhesive plastic figures (in gold at first, then grey and subsequently black) replaced the pressed plates and depot identification was by means of one or two coloured discs in the same material placed above the fleet numbers as follows:

Eastern area	
Southampton	Yellow
Fareham	Yellow and black
Winchester	Yellow and orange
Woolston	Yellow and pink
Eastleigh	Yellow and grey
Northern area	
Salisbury	Blue
Basingstoke	Blue and black
Andover	Blue and orange
Amesbury	Blue and pink
Pewsey	Blue and grey

Above: Bodywork by Brush was featured on most single- and double-deck vehicles purchased between 1933 and 1938 as exemplified by No. **973** (**LJ 9404**), a 1934 Leyland Titan TD3 seen at Southampton early in 1951. Note the separate number box which was a later addition.

Below: In the mid-1930s, the Company purchased a small number of Leyland Cub and Dennis Ace vehicles for rural services. An example of the latter with Harrington 20-seat body dating from 1934 is seen at Southampton in the early 1950s after withdrawal. *(Both: Solent Transport Trust)*

Western area

Poole	White
Bournemouth	White and black
Lymington	White and orange
Ringwood	White and pink
Blandford	White and grey
Swanage	White and brown

Those for Woolston, Ringwood, Blandford and Amesbury were in use for only a few months, as these depots closed in February the following year, although Blandford and Ringwood remained as outstations. The above was preparatory for the October 1972 change when the Wilts & Dorset fleet was fully merged with that of Hants & Dorset. A total of 282 vehicles was involved, mostly Bristol double-deckers and saloons with ECW bodies dating from 1952 onwards and Bedford coaches with Duple bodies built from 1965 to 1971. There was also a solitary Harrington-bodied Leyland L1 Leopard which had been acquired with the business of Silver Star of Porton Down by Wilts & Dorset in 1963 and 16 Willowbrook-bodied Leyland Panther saloons which were Wilts & Dorset's share of the 33 such vehicles acquired by Hants & Dorset from Maidstone and District in 1971/2. The Wilts & Dorset fleet numbers below 1000 were retained. Fifteen withdrawn vehicles were also transferred from the Wilts & Dorset fleet, but these did not see further service. From October 1972, all vehicles in the combined fleet carried the Hants & Dorset fleet name, although by now no longer in the traditional style, but to the National Bus Company's corporate design, while the NBC's poppy-red livery gradually replaced the existing Tilling green (Hants & Dorset) and Tilling red (Wilts & Dorset) liveries.

New and acquired vehicles from 1st January 1973 were numbered from 3001 upwards using the same hundred blocks per vehicle type introduced in 1971:

3001 - 3099	Coaches (including second-hand)
3301 - 3456	Bristol VRT double-deckers
3482 - 3499	Bristol LD, LDS, FS and FSF Lodekkas hired and acquired
3501 - 3599	Bristol LH and Ford R1014 saloons
3601 - 3751	Leyland National saloons
3801 - 3816	Bristol LH and Ford R1014 saloons
3817 - 3858	Bristol LH saloons acquired from Bristol Omnibus in 1981/2
3899	Bristol MW coach acquired from Lincolnshire Road Car in 1973
3995 - 3999	Leyland Atlanteans from Maidstone & District in 1973

On 29th April 1973 the well-known business of R Chisnell & Sons Limited of Winchester, who had traded as 'King Alfred' since 1921, was purchased. The fleet was renumbered into the 2000 series and consisted of Leyland, Bedford and Metro-Scania saloons, AEC and Leyland double-deckers, four Bedford coaches and seven Ford Transit minibuses. The King Alfred emblem on the vehicles soon gave way to the Hants & Dorset fleetname and the original two-tone green livery was subsequently replaced by the National Bus Company poppy-red, with the exception of the four AEC Bridgemasters, the two Bedford saloons and the three Metro-Scanias. The Metro-Scanias were later exchanged for three dual-door Leyland National saloons from London Country in October 1973.

The 1970s saw a large intake of acquired vehicles to cover a shortage of buses and coaches. In addition to the Leyland Panthers from Maidstone & District already mentioned, there were Leyland Leopard coaches from North Western (in 1973/5), Southdown (in 1974/7/81) and Ribble (in 1977/8); Bristol LD5G Lodekkas from Eastern National (in 1973/4), Bristol LDS, FS and FSF Lodekkas from Southdown (in 1974/5) and Ford saloons from Potteries and Southdown (in 1980/1). Hired vehicles were a common sight during this period, especially in 1973-5 when there were Bristol LD Lodekkas from Southern Vectis, AEC Swifts from Southampton Corporation, Daimler Roadliners and Leyland PD2s from Bournemouth Corporation, AEC Regents from Devon General and Leyland Atlanteans from Portsmouth Corporation on loan to Hants & Dorset. Their different liveries certainly added a colourful touch to the Hants & Dorset scene. In January 1974, the Company acquired the Swanage area services and the following vehicles from Western National:

Above: Among the coaches acquired from Elliott Brothers (Royal Blue) of Bournemouth in 1935 were four of the then revolutionary AEC Q type with side engine mounted behind the offside front wheel. Three (LJ 8001, 8600/1) had Duple coachwork, including No. **Q440** (**LJ 8600**), seen here at Bournemouth in 1949. *(John Banks Collection)*

Below: The Q types had been new between November 1933 and June 1934. This postwar view, taken at Bristol, shows the newest of them, **Q446** (**AEL 2**), which had a Harrington 35-seat centre-entrance body. *(Bristol Vintage Bus Group)*

1742/54/68	RTT 952/73/87	Bristol
	LS5G ECW B41F new 1955	
1779/80	TUO 495/6	Bristol
	LS5G ECW B41F new 1956	
1652	LDV 459F	Bristol
	RELL6G ECW B53F new 68	

The fleet numbers shown are those used by Hants & Dorset, those of the LSs also being the former Western National fleet numbers. Also during 1974, the Company took delivery of ten ECW-bodied Bristol LH6Ls numbered 3530-9 (ORU 530-9M), which were built with a portion of their front panelling cut away in order to improve clearance on the approach ramps to the Sandbanks - Shell Bay car ferry. The front overhang on the LH is proportionally longer to the rest of the vehicle, while the rear overhang is short enough not to require any modifications unlike earlier vehicles adapted for use on the ferry.

A disastrous fire struck the two-level Bournemouth bus and coach station in July 1976, with the loss of 18 Hants & Dorset and National Travel coaches, including Hants & Dorset's two ECW-bodied Bristol RELHs (AEL 6/7B). The whole of the lower coach operating area and much of the upper Hants & Dorset area was beyond economic repair and Hants & Dorset transferred most of its operations to roadside stands in the nearby Triangle area of Bournemouth, ironically just around the corner from the company's original headquarters in Norwich Avenue, which it was soon to re-acquire. Depot facilities were provided by Bournemouth Corporation Transport at its Mallard Road depot. Hants & Dorset hired four coaches from Southdown as temporary replacements for its fire victims including 2728 CD, a Harrington-bodied Leyland Leopard of 1961 which was painted in the original two-tone green livery complete with original-style scroll fleetname.

The Market Analysis Project (MAP) which had been used throughout much of the NBC was introduced in 1978. This was designed to provide a more economic use of vehicles and services operated by Hants & Dorset. With the revised services came local fleet names such as 'Wiltsway' (for Salisbury and Pewsey area services) and 'South Wessex' (for Poole and Bournemouth area services). These names were

carried on the buses in addition to the plain white Hants & Dorset name. Evening and Sunday services bore the brunt of the revisions, but there were also frequency reductions at other times. One result of the MAP project was the final withdrawal of crew- (i.e. driver and conductor) operated vehicles from the fleet. The last such bus, a half-cab rear-entrance Bristol FL Lodekka (1210, 7685 LJ) operated the Poole, Wimborne and Bournemouth service on 29th November 1980. The same date also saw the last Bournemouth-based bus enter Bournemouth bus station (in the early hours of the following morning), as Bournemouth depot was closed from that date. In May 1981, the tours and express services of Shamrock & Rambler, together with 37 Leyland Leopard coaches, which carried a mixture of 11- and 12-metre bodies by Plaxton, Willowbrook or Duple and two 12-metre Duple AEC Reliances, as well as the premises in Holdenhurst Road, Bournemouth, passed from the control of National Travel (South West) to that of Hants & Dorset. This was the first time in its history that Hants & Dorset had control of express services, but the Shamrock & Rambler fleet name was retained. Also in May 1981 the company's new Central Repair Works, located in part of the former carriage works of British Rail at Eastleigh, was officially opened. This facility replaced two separate locations in Southampton at Winchester Road and Shirley Road. A month later, Hants & Dorset finally vacated the bus station building in Exeter Road, Bournemouth, and the headquarters was transferred to a five-storey building in Oxford Road, Bournemouth adjacent to the rear of the Shamrock & Rambler premises recently acquired.

At the other end of the company's operations, MAP had resulted in the operations from the Fareham depot being marketed as 'New Provincial' from June 1980 and integrated with the services of the Gosport & Fareham Omnibus Company (generally known by its 'Provincial' fleet name) which was based at Hoeford. Once again, green buses were using Fareham bus station!

A final, and terminal, reorganisation as far as the Hants & Dorset company was concerned took place in April 1983 as part of the preparation for the deregulation of bus services in the United Kingdom and as a prelude to the

Above: Nine Leyland LT5A Lions with Brush 34-seat front-entrance bodies were delivered in March 1935. **BA212 (ALJ 790)** is seen here in Fareham bus station in this prewar view with in the background the Methodist Chapel, which was demolished in the 1950s to allow the bus station to be extended. *(Bob Rowe Collection)*

Below: Fourteen Leyland TS7s with Beadle 32-seat coach bodies were purchased in 1935 and all were requisitioned by the War Department in 1940. In 1948 Hants & Dorset reacquired three of these buses and had them rebodied with 32-seat dual-purpose bodies by Portsmouth Aviation Coachworks, as shown here by **726 (ARU 174)**, seen at Southampton in March 1954. *(P F Davies)*

privatisation of the National Bus Company. A separate engineering company was formed, as tended to be the fashion at the time, and operations were divided into four new companies. The western and northern area buses, which had of course been painted red since 1972, finally assumed the more appropriate (as far as the livery was concerned) fleet name of the resurrected Wilts & Dorset company, with the exception of the Basingstoke depot, which together with the remains of the eastern area (Fareham excepted), became the Hampshire Bus Company Limited. The Fareham operation was finally completely merged with the Provincial company and in due course was privatised through an employee's buy-out as 'Peoples Provincial'. The coaching division became a separate company, Shamrock and Rambler Coaches Ltd. The Wilts & Dorset Bus Company succumbed to a management buy-out in 1987, and Hampshire Bus was sold to the Stagecoach group. The almost immediate closure of the long established Southampton bus station at West Marlands led to murmurings of asset-stripping and a feeling by some that this was what deregulation was really about. What was clear was that the last links with W W Graham's pioneering company had finally disappeared, only to be remembered in a tribute such as this publication.

The Hants & Dorset operating area as it stood in April 1935. *(Bob Rowe Collection)*

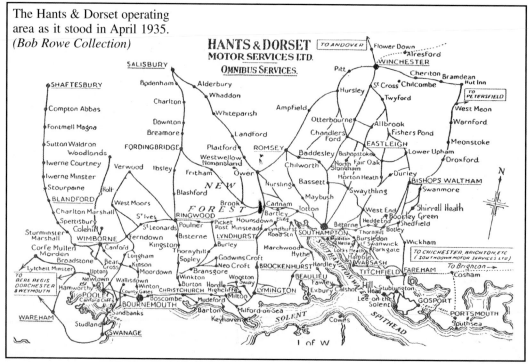

Above: Also in 1935, Hants & Dorset acquired the tours and excursions licences, together with eleven coaches, of Tourist Motor Coaches of Southampton. Hants & Dorset fleet number **F496** (**TR 6166**), a Leyland Tiger TS2 of 1929, was rebodied with this Beadle 28-seat body in 1937 and is seen here at Epsom in 1948 after having been fitted with a "Coventry" conversion radiator. Note the hinged streamlined fairing between the canopy and the nearside front wing. *(Alan B Cross)*

Below: Two unidentified Leyland Tigers carrying similar coachwork by Beadle feature in this view taken on the Isle of Wight. The vehicles had gone over to the Island on day trip excursions. *(John Banks Collection)*

Above: Eighteen Leyland TD4c chassis with Brush 52-seat lowbridge bodies were purchased to replace the Bournemouth trams on the Upper Parkstone route to Poole in 1935. The torque-converter transmissions were subsequently replaced by ordinary gearboxes. Number **995** (**BEL 391**) is seen here with Blackwell of Earls Colne to whom it was sold in 1951. *(P F Davies Collection)*

Below: Number **1003** (**BLJ 994**), a 1936 Titan TD4, also bodied by Brush, was rebuilt by Portsmouth Aviation Coachworks in 1949 and is seen here at Eastleigh in 1954. Note the deep sliding vents. *(R H G Simpson)*

Above: Similar vehicle No. **1004** (**BLJ 995**) was less extensively rebuilt, and by Hants & Dorset rather than an outside coachbuilder, in 1947 as shown by this view at Southampton in 1954 after the vehicle had been withdrawn. *(Solent Transport Trust)*

Below: Hants & Dorset adopted the Royal Blue livery and fleet name of Elliott Brothers of Bournemouth when the tours and excursions were acquired in 1935. This livery was also applied to new coaches bought in 1935/6 including **L452** (**CEL 223**), a Leyland KPZ2 Cub with 20-seat Beadle coachwork, dating from 1936. *(P F Davies Collection)*

Above: Fleet number **644** (**CCR 856**), a 1939 Leyland Cub KPZ4, one of a pair delivered in that year with similar Beadle 20-seat coachwork, is seen at Royal Pier, Southampton, in the mid 1950s, not long before its withdrawal from service in November 1956. Its original Leyland 4.7-litre petrol engine had been replaced by a Leyland diesel unit of the same capacity in 1950. *(David Burnicle)*

Below: The New Forest near Lyndhurst provides the scene for this 1936 Leyland TS7 with Beadle C28F body on an afternoon tour from Bournemouth. **F456** (**CEL 225**) is seen here in the green and cream coach livery introduced in 1937. *(Hants & Dorset)*

Above: In 1937 Hants & Dorset bought two Dennis Ace saloons with 20-seat Mumford bodies, which were part of a diverted Southern and Western National order. Both vehicles were converted to tree loppers in 1950 and No. **539** (**CTA 518**) is seen here as such in the Bath Road garage, Bournemouth, in 1963. *(P F Davies)*

Below: Hants & Dorset's first Bristols arrived in 1938 and No. **1015** (**BTR 305**), a K5G with Brush 54-seat body, is seen here at Winchester depot in 1950 in company with three other Bristols. *(Bristol Vintage Bus Group)*

Above: Number **1015** (**BTR 305**) is seen again having had its Brush lowbridge body extensively rebuilt by Hants & Dorset in 1951. A postwar-style low radiator and deep cab windscreen were fitted at the same time. A 1959 Southampton post-withdrawal view.

Below: In 1954 Hants & Dorset had ten prewar Bristol K5G chassis rebodied with new Eastern Coach Works 60-seat highbridge bodies of the style normally associated with the KSW chassis. Six of these, including **1013** (**BTR 303**), were convertible to open-top and were painted in cream livery. It is seen here at Lee-on-Solent. *(Both: Solent Transport Trust)*

Two versions of the Beadle-bodied Bristol L5Gs dating from 1938-40. In the view above No. **755** (**ERU 519**) demonstrates the original half-canopy style and side indicator. Number **734** (**BOW 167**) *(below)* shows the full-width canopy and large indicator display as rebuilt by Hants & Dorset in 1950. Both vehicles have the cut away rear panelling, enabling them to use the Sandbanks - Shell Bay ferry. *(Both: Solent Transport Trust)*

Above: Two Bristol L5Gs from 1938/9 are seen here at Bournemouth bus station in March 1954. On the left is No. **737** (**BOW 170**) with the original front-entrance Beadle body; and on the right is No. **745** (**EEL 807**) with a rear entrance 32-seat Beadle body built in 1947 and transferred from a 1930 Leyland LT1 chassis in 1951. *(P F Davies)*

Below: Eastern Coach Works bodies first made their appearance in the Hants & Dorset fleet on 1939 Bristol K5G chassis and one such example was No. **1041** (**ERU 592**), a lowbridge 53-seater. It is seen here at the Grosvenor Square, Southampton, depot in 1952. *(Solent Transport Trust)*

Above: Another Bristol K5G with ECW 53-seat body was No. **1064** (**AFX 761**), which was rebuilt by Hants & Dorset with a low radiator and more vertical front end styling in 1952. Seven years later 1064 was converted for driver-training use, as seen in this view. *(R F Mack)*

Below: An early example of the Cave-Browne-Cave heating and ventilating system was fitted to No. **1068** (**APR 423**), a 1940 Bristol K5G with ECW 53-seat body rebuilt by Hants & Dorset. The Lodekka style bonnet and cowl was fitted in 1955 to enclose an engine supercharger which was fitted for a time, and 1068 is seen here in this guise descending Bath Hill, Bournemouth in 1957. *(P F Davies Collection)*

Above: Number **1069** (**APR 424**), a 1940 Bristol K5G, received this body from sister vehicle 1085 (FLJ 537) in late 1954; the body was rebuilt on transfer to include sliding side vents. The original high-mounted radiator was retained, as can be seen in this 1958 view at Southampton depot. This batch of vehicles, (1065-77, APR 420-32), were the last to be registered by the Company with Dorset County Council. The policy of registering new vehicles in one or other of Bournemouth (EL, LJ or RU), Dorset (FX, JT, PR or TK) or Southampton (OW or TR) went back to the earliest days of Hants & Dorset. *(P F Davies)*

Below: On the left is No. **1084** (**FLJ 536**), another 1940 Bristol K5G, with ECW 53-seat body rebuilt by Hants & Dorset on transfer from a 1939 K5G chassis in early 1954. Note the Auster-type upper saloon front vents. On the right is a 1938 Bristol K5G, **1026** (**JT 9354**) with a low radiator and 1949 ECW 55-seat body. The non standard-indicator is of interest. *(Solent Transport Trust)*

Above: In 1942/3 Hants & Dorset was allocated nine Guy Arabs with utility bodies, including these two Strachan-bodied examples. The body of No. **1099** (**FRU 9**) was rebuilt by Reading of Portsmouth in 1948.

Below: Number **1098** (**FRU 8**) was more extensively rebuilt in 1949, but this time by Portsmouth Aviation. *(Both: R Sinclair Collection)*

Upper: In 1952/3 Hants & Dorset constructed fully fronted open-top bodies utilising parts from Brush and Strachan bodies in their works and placed them on 1938 and 1945 Bristol K chassis. Number **1111** (**FRU 308**), a 1945 Bristol K6A with the earlier six-bay body, is seen in Christchurch on its way to New Milton. The common haunt of these buses was service 6 to Sandbanks, but they also operated on the 218. *(Bob Rowe)*

Centre: Number **1011** (**BTR 301**), a 1938 Bristol K5G, had the later five-bay body structure with 'standee' windows and is seen here at Bournemouth bus station in 1956. *(John C Gillham)*

Lower: The earliest of the postwar ECW bodies incorporated square-cornered sliding vents as exemplified by this 55-seat lowbridge body on a 1946 Bristol K5G chassis. **1115** (**FRU 826**) was at Gosport in this mid 1950s view. *(R Sinclair Collection)*

>> *Opposite page:* Number **1116** (**FRU 827**) was another 1946 Bristol K5G, but the six-bay ECW body dates from 1940 and was rebuilt by Hants & Dorset on transfer from its original K5G chassis, No. 1077 (APR 432), in early 1956. In 1964 the vehicle was converted to a driver trainer, as shown in this view at Southampton. The body was no fewer than 32 years old by the time of its withdrawal in 1972. *(Solent Transport Trust)*

NOT ON SERVICE
DRIVER UNDER
INSTRUCTION

DRIVERS TRAINING BUS

New! Esso

L DRIVER
UNDER
INSTRUCTION

FRU 827

35

Above: This view of **TC815** (**GRU 859**), a 1947 Bristol L6G with Beadle 28-seat coachwork, clearly shows the handsome and dignified green and cream coach livery which was introduced in 1937. *(Hants & Dorset)*

Below: As a consequence of the general shortage of buses in the period of austerity in the early postwar years Hants & Dorset, in common with certain other former Tilling Group companies, accepted chassis of non-Bristol manufacture. Among these were seven Leyland PD1A Titans with 53-seat lowbridge bodies by ECW. This batch of buses spent most of its life allocated to Winchester depot, where No. **1150** (**GLJ 962**) is seen in the late 1950s. *(Bob Rowe Collection)*

Above: London Transport also suffered a vehicle shortage in the late 1940s and many new Bristol/Eastern Coach Works vehicles intended for British Transport Commission former Tilling Group companies were delivered on loan directly to London, remaining there from late 1948 until early 1950. Among these were 39 Hants & Dorset lowbridge Bristol K6As, TD876-914. **TD895 (HLJ 44)** is seen in the Capital and it went to its rightful owner in March 1950 as No. 1187, under the fleet-numbering scheme introduced on 1st January that year. In preservation for some years, this bus has been restored to its 'on loan to London' condition. *(Alan B Cross)*

Below: A 1948 example of the early postwar Eastern Coach Works 35-seat rear-entrance saloon body is shown mounted on a Bristol L6A chassis. Number **773 (HLJ 47)** was resting between duties at Winchester depot around 1960. *(P F Davies Collection)*

Above: Number **652** (**HRU 365**), a 1948 Bristol L6B with Beadle 31-seat coach body, is seen here in original form in the Bristol area in 1953. It was working on day tour excursion duties. *(Bristol Vintage Bus Group)*

Below: The same bus is seen here after conversion by Hants & Dorset in 1957 with a full-width front for one-man operation. The coach seats had been retained. It was photographed outside Eastleigh depot later that year. *(P F Davies)*

Above: Uncommon makes of coachwork were to be found on Bristol chassis in the Hants & Dorset fleet. Number **657** (**HRU 455**) was a 1948 L6B with Dutfield half-canopy-style body. It is pictured at Bournemouth bus station in July 1954.

Below: Portsmouth Aviation Coachworks built this 32-seat rear-entrance coach body on a Bristol L6A chassis. Registered **JRU 67**, fleet number **664** is seen inside Southampton depot in September 1958. (*Both: P F Davies*)

Above: Before 1952 highbridge bodies were rare in the Hants & Dorset fleet, but in 1949 six Leyland-bodied 56-seat Titan PD2/1s were delivered, part of an order diverted from South Africa. By the time this photograph of No. **1224** (**JEL 501**) was taken at Southampton in June 1960, the company had replaced the original half-drop windows with sliding ones. These buses were generally to be found operating on the Southampton-Fawley service. *(P F Davies)*

Below: AECs were also rare in the Hants & Dorset fleet. Number **1215** (**JEL 754**) was one of six Regent llls with Northern Counties 53-seat lowbridge bodies diverted from Western SMT in 1949 and is seen at Bournemouth bus station in April 1962. These AECs did at least share the same engine as that fitted to the Bristol K6A; at the time the Regents were delivered to Hants & Dorset, their own AEC-engined Bristols were on loan to London Transport. *(Bob Rowe Collection)*

Above: Bristol double-deckers returned to the Hants & Dorset scene from late 1949. This view at the former Towngate Street depot in Poole shows Nos **1252** (**JEL 271**), a 1950 K5G on the left, and **1292** (**KRU 958**), a 1951 KSW6B. The 55-seat ECW body is common to both but the extra six inches on the KSW is readily apparent.

Below: A wet February scene at Southampton in 1966 shows two 1950 Bristol K6Bs with ECW 55-seat lowbridge bodies. Number **1267** (**KEL710**) is on the left; on the right sister vehicle **1258** (**KEL 701**) had had its indicator layout modified. *(Both: P F Davies)*

Above: A batch of 18 Bristol L6Gs with elegant Portsmouth Aviation Coachworks 28-seat coach bodies was delivered in 1950. They were mainly used on extended holiday tours in their early years although No. **667** (**KEL 62**) is seen in 1951 on hire to Associated Motorways, in all probability on a busy summer Saturday working. *(Bristol Vintage Bus Group)*

Below: Most of the 1950 Bristol L6Gs were transformed in 1959-62 by lengthening the chassis and replacing the Portsmouth Aviation coach bodies with new 30ft-long fully fronted ECW saloon bodies. Number **679** (**KEL 407**), thus rebodied and with its chassis now to LL6B specification, was climbing the steep hill out of Swanage towards Durlston Castle in August 1969. *(P F Davies)*

Above: The chassis of No. **781** (**KLJ 751**) was the only Bristol LWL6G built for the British home market. The Portsmouth Aviation Coachworks dual-purpose 36-seat rear-entrance body was also the last to be painted in the elaborate green and cream coach livery. This 1951 photograph shows the darker shade of green applied to wings, wheels and side flash.

Below: Between November 1951 and May 1953 no fewer than 38 Bristol KSWs with ECW 60-seat highbridge bodies were delivered to the Company. The majority was allocated to Poole depot for local town services; but some of the later KSW6Gs operated from Southampton, Fareham and Winchester depots. This October 1973 view shows a 1952 KSW6B, No. **1384** (formerly 1321 - **KRU 987**) working a Winchester city service following the acquisition of R Chisnell & Sons (King Alfred) earlier in 1973. *(Both: Bristol Vintage Bus Group)*

Above: Seven Bristol LL6Bs with ECW 39-seat rear-entrance bodies were delivered in late 1951 and early 1952. Between 1959 and 1962 Hants & Dorset converted all these vehicles to front-entrance specification and fitted full-width cabs to make them suitable for one-man operation. Number **785** (**KRU 991**) is seen in Southampton in 1964. A Gardner 5LW engine had replaced the original Bristol AVW unit in this vehicle as early as February 1953.

Below: The first coaches in cream livery with light-green wings and wheels came in 1951: Bristol LL6B (but with 8ft-wide bodies) and LWL6B chassis and 35-seat ECW bodies. They quickly attracted the soubriquet 'Queen Mary' in deference to the liner of the same name which by this time was operating a regular transatlantic service from Southampton docks. This view taken at Bournemouth bus station in May 1964 shows No. **696** (**KRU 997**) in green livery after conversion for one-man operation in December 1963. The sliding vents had replaced the original winding windows in December 1957. *(Both: P F Davies)*

Above: The underfloor-engined Bristol LS made its debut in the Hants & Dorset fleet early in 1953. The 43-seat ECW saloon bodies had front and rear doors. From 1958 the rear doorway was removed, without an increase in seating capacity, making them suitable for one-man operation. The first of these saloons was No. **789** (**MLJ 141**), seen here at Bramdean on the Winchester to Petersfield service in July 1969, by which time its days with Hants & Dorset were numbered. *(P F Davies)*

Below: The first batch of Bristol LS6G/ECW coaches, delivered in 1953, had outward opening doors as shown in this view of No. **699** (**MLJ 144**) taken in Southampton coach station in about 1961. Between 1953 and 1959 these coaches had been used on extended holiday tours with reclining seats for only 28 passengers - later increased to 30. *(J Kirby)*

Above: Hants & Dorset received one of the six pre-production series Lodekkas in 1953. Number **1337** (**LRU 67**) was an LD6B with 58-seat body and is seen at Keyhaven in July 1966. Note the deeper grille and cowl with which these early Lodekkas were fitted and which 1337 retained until withdrawal in 1975. *(Bob Rowe)*

Below: Number **1351** (**NEL 27**) was a 58-seat Bristol LD6G Lodekka dating from 1954. This early 1960s view was taken at Woolston bus station, situated next to the depot, which was closed in February 1972. The shipyards of Vosper Thornycroft loom in the background and also close by at this fascinating location was the terminus of the floating bridge to Southampton, which itself was replaced in 1977 by the new Itchen Bridge. *(Solent Transport Trust)*

Above: Hants & Dorset's second batch of Bristol LS6Gs, with ECW 39-seat coach bodies, had the more familiar frontal styling with inward opening door. Number **857** (**SRU 971**), dating from 1956, is seen at Southampton bus station in 1964. *(P F Davies)*

Below: Photographed in Stubbington in April 1973 and carrying its new fleet number, depot identification marks and NBC logo, No. **1788** (ex-802 - **SRU 978**) is *en route* to Gosport. Service 93 was normally operated at this time by double-deckers, but this afternoon short working from Titchfield tended to utilise saloons. *(Bob Rowe)*

Above: The underfloor-engined Bristol LS and MW coaches made for easier conversion to stage carriage specification than had earlier front-engined types. Here we see No. **862 (UEL 736)**, a 1957 LS6G rebuilt by Hants & Dorset in 1967.

Below: The Bristol MW had replaced the LS in 1958; the latter had been an integral chassisless design, whereas the former reverted to having a separate chassis. Number **865 (YEL 224)**, a 1959 MW6G, was converted for stage-carriage work in 1967 and is seen here crossing a ford at Moyles Court in 1969. Service 119, on which it is seen operating, ran on Wednesdays and Saturdays only between Ringwood and Fordingbridge. *(Both: P F Davies)*

Above: Hants & Dorset were allocated one of the six experimental 30ft-long Bristol LDL Lodekkas in late 1957. Number **1406** (**UEL 727**) is seen with its original open platform opposite the Company's main works at Southampton in 1958. The 70-seat ECW body was fitted with driver-controlled platform doors by Hants & Dorset in 1962.

Below: By 1961 most of the former Tilling group fleets were meeting their requirements for 70-seat double-deckers with the forward-entrance FLF Lodekka. Hants & Dorset was one of the few companies which continued to favour the rear-entrance version of this high capacity vehicle and thus ordered six Bristol/ECW FL model Lodekkas in each of 1961 (with Bristol engines) and 1962 (Gardner-engined). Number **1466** (**4389 LJ**), one of the 1961 FL6Bs, is seen here on the Southampton to Hamble service near Bursledon in 1969. *(Both: P F Davies)*

Above: The shorter and more familiar FS-type rear-entrance Lodekka is depicted here in the form of No. **1450** (**5677 EL**), an FS6G which was delivered in 1961. *(Solent Transport Trust)*

Below: The 1962 deliveries were FS6Bs (i.e. with Bristol engines rather than Gardner) and also had the revised grille introduced that year. Number **1479** (**7679 LJ**) is seen near the Potteries Junction in 1968 following the route of the former tram service from Bournemouth to Poole via Lower Parkstone. *(P F Davies)*

Above: Numbers 882-7 (7118-23 LJ), delivered in May and June 1962 brought into the fleet the first examples of the new Eastern Coach Works body design - the first major redesign from ECW since its first coachwork for underfloor-engined chassis in 1952/3. Two of the six 39-seat Bristol MW6Gs, Nos **884/5 (7120/1 LJ)**, were photographed on holiday tour work in 1963.

Below: The 36ft-long coach was introduced to the Hants & Dorset fleet in 1964 in the shape of two rear-engined Bristol RELH6Gs with 47-seat ECW bodies. Number 898, as renumbered **1052** in 1971 (**AEL 7B**), is seen in Newcastle in 1975 shortly after repaint into National Bus Company "local coach" livery. *(Both: Geoff Coxon)*

Above: The first Limited Stop service was launched in 1965. Bristol Lodekka No. **1511** (**BRU 141B**), a Bournemouth allocation, stands in Southampton bus station awaiting return to its home town. *(Bob Rowe)*

Below: Hants & Dorset eventually took delivery of the forward-entrance FLF Lodekka in 1965. Number **1517** (**CLJ 868C**), an FLF6B with 70-seat ECW body, was photographed at Ferndown in March 1965 during its first month in service. *(P F Davies)*

Above: The last Hants & Dorset Bristol MWs delivered to the company were five MW6Gs in 1966 and were unusual among later examples of this chassis in having five-cylinder Gardner engines. Number **1856** (**HEL 390D**) is seen at Winchester bus station in 1972 and is equipped to carry boats on the roof in connection with certain private hire requirements. *(B H Botley)*

Below: Between 1967 and 1969 Hants & Dorset purchased Duple-bodied Bristol REs for its coach fleet. Number **1024** (**JEL 423E**) is an example of the rare, shorter RESH chassis with 36-seat Duple Commander ll body. The photograph was taken in Bournemouth bus station. *(T Dayman)*

Above: The longer and more common RELH type is illustrated here by No. **1054** (**MRU 126F**), also at Bournemouth bus station in about 1972. Coachwork was by Duple to Commander III design. *(T Dayman)*

Below: This combination of handsome Duple coachwork and the rear-engined Bristol RE chassis was never common and a sighting of one in "foreign parts" was always an event. Here, in National all-over white coaching livery, is No. **1054** again, photographed in 1975 outside Newcastle Central railway station. *(Geoff Coxon)*

Above: In early 1968 Hants & Dorset purchased four 1953 Bristol/ECW LS6B coaches from Southern Vectis and immediately converted them for use on stage-carriage work as one-man saloons. These were the only Bristol-engined LSs in the fleet and three of them were subsequently fitted with Gardner 5HLW units. Number **845** (**JDL 758**) is seen here as an LS5G on the Royal Pier to Central Station service in Southampton in July 1969.

Below: By 1964, Hants & Dorset had secured an all-Bristol fleet and this was to last until 1967 when, because of supply problems at Bristol, demand could not be met and Hants & Dorset took into stock 15 lightweight Bedfords with either Strachan or Willowbrook bodies. Number **3007** (**MRU 70F**) was a Bedford VAM with a Willowbrook 40-seat dual-doorway body and is pictured at Almer on the Blandford to Bere Regis service in March 1969. *(Both: P F Davies)*

Above: The Bristol option for a lightweight bus was the LH and Hants & Dorset No. **828** (**NLJ 817G**) was an LH6L model (and thus Leyland-engined) with an ECW 39-seat dual-doorway body. It was at Woolston depot (hitherto an all-double-deck garage) on its first day in service in January 1969. This vehicle was the first of many LHs bought by the Company. Note the shallow windscreen and side ventilators compared with later models of this type.

Below: By contrast, the heavyweight rear-engined Bristol RELL6G saloon entered the fleet in late 1968, but these were purchased primarily as replacements for double-deckers. An early example was No. **835** (**NLJ 824G**) with 45-seat dual-door ECW body seen at Bournemouth bus station in December 1968. *(Both: P F Davies)*

Above: By way of contrast, No. **840** (**NLJ 829G**) had 50 semi-coach seats in a single-doorway body and was painted in dual-purpose livery. It features in another Bournemouth bus station scene. *(P F Davies)*

Below: Number **1617** (ex-3011 - **PLJ 742G**) was another RELL6G with 45-seat dual-door body but had the taller windscreen introduced in mid-1969. It is seen at Southampton in 1971. *(T Dayman)*

Above: The first lightweight coach to be purchased during the 1969-71 period was No. **1056** (**ORU 579G**), a twin-steer Bedford VAL with 49-seat Duple Viceroy coachwork which, in this view, is in the NBC's poppy-red and white dual-purpose livery, otherwise sometimes known as the 'local coach' livery.

Below: The last two Bristol coaches purchased by the company had appropriate registration marks. RELH6G No. **1057** (ex-924) carried **REL 741H** and was fitted with air suspension and a 40-seat Duple Commander IV body. Delivered in August 1969, it is illustrated in NBC white livery by which time its seating capacity had been increased to 49. *(Both: M Wort)*

Above: In June 1971, six Daimler Fleetlines with Roe 74-seat highbridge bodies were diverted to Hants & Dorset from the Gosport and Fareham Omnibus Company in exchange for six new Bristol RELL saloons. Four entered service in Poole, but two initially went to Southampton depot where No. **1906** (**VRU 129J**) is seen on service 54 with the imposing Civic Centre in the background. These six vehicles were the first to be issued with fleet numbers under the 1971 renumbering scheme, which was not introduced for the rest of the fleet until September. *(Bob Rowe)*

Below: In October 1972 the Wilts & Dorset fleet was merged with that of Hants & Dorset. One of the vehicles transferred was No. **928** (**SLJ 756H**), a 1970 Bedford VAL70 with Duple Viceroy 37 49-seat front-entrance coachwork. Newcastle-upon-Tyne was one of the destinations for the weekend leave services for troops stationed on Salisbury Plain. Such services had been a feature of the operations of Silver Star Services, acquired by Wilts & Dorset seven years earlier. *(S J Kelly)*

Above: New Hants & Dorset vehicles in 1971 were a mixed batch: Bristol RELL6G and LHL6L models, Daimler Fleetlines, Bedford VAL70s and a trio of Plaxton-bodied Leyland Leopards, two of which are seen at Blackpool in 1975. Numbers **1061/2** (**WEL 464/7J**) were PSU3B/4R models with 40-seat coachwork.

Below: An interesting event in January 1973 was the purchase from the North Western Road Car Company, of Stockport, of five 1966 Leyland PSU4/4R Leopards with Duple Northern 41-seat coachwork. From the batch FJA 225-9D, to which Hants & Dorset allocated fleet numbers 3001-5, we illustrate No. **3005** (**FJA 229D**). *(Both: Geoff Coxon)*

Above: Four Bedford coaches were among the vehicles included in the sale to Hants & Dorset of the King Alfred business on 29th April 1973. One of these was **EOU 703D**, which Hants & Dorset numbered 2052, a VAL model with Plaxton 49-seat body that had been new in 1966. A rather fine model of sister vehicle CCG 704C was produced by Corgi in 2001. *(S J Kelly)*

Below: Among the influx of second-hand coaches bought in to combat a serious shortage of serviceable stock in the seventies were some Leyland Leopards from Ribble Motor Services in 1977 and 1979. One of the 1977 intake, No. **3086** (**CRN 832D**), was photographed in that year closer to its original home than to its new: it was on the forecourt of the Gallowgate, Newcastle, depot of United Automobile Services. *(Geoff Coxon)*

Above: In March 1973 Hants & Dorset acquired six 1960 Leyland Atlanteans with 77-seat highbridge MCW bodies from Maidstone & District. Only five entered service and the first to do so were Nos **3998/9 (556/67 LKP)** at Southampton in February 1974, where they are seen after having been painted in NBC poppy-red livery and converted for one-man operation.

Below: A sign of the times in March 1974: 43-seat Bristol MW6G No. **838 (EMR 303D)** retains its Wilts & Dorset fleetname on the front but the Hants & Dorset fleet name is also present on the vehicle as it traverses Savernake Forest on the Marlborough to Great Bedwyn service. *(Both: P F Davies)*

Above: Bournemouth bus station from the Company's offices on 24th April 1973. Over four years into the National Bus Company, everything seems reassuringly traditional, but NBC-style "double-N" logos and fleetnames are evident and the next handful of years would bring immense change, not uniformly for the better.

Below: Hants & Dorset's first rear-engined Bristol VRT double-deckers with ECW bodies arrived in December 1972. The six vehicles concerned became 3301-6 (CRU 301-6L) and entered service at Basingstoke depot in January 1973, although not before one of them, initially numbered 1304 (CRU 304L), had been used at Poole depot immediately after delivery. Number **3306 (CRU 306L)** is seen here at its home depot in September that year. *(Both: Bob Rowe)*

Above: Number **3384** (**URU 691S**), a Bristol VRT/SL3/6LXB with the usual ECW 74-seat coachwork, typifies the all-over-advertisement treatment that became very popular following London Transport's pioneering Silexine Paints Routemaster. URU 691S was new in 1977 and photographed the following year. It was transferred to Wilts & Dorset on 1st April 1983 and then in September 1997 to ... Hants & Dorset - but not the Hants & Dorset we have been discussing: this late use of the name was by Damory Coaches, of Blandford. The vehicle is believed to be still in service at the time of writing (late July 2005).

Below: As an NBC operator, Hants & Dorset could not escape the Leyland National phenomenon. In a variation on the advertising theme, No. **3737** (**XFX 898S**), a 1978 Type 11351A/1R, has extensive, but not quite all-over, dedicated advertising. Also transferred to Wilts & Dorset in April 1983, it was sold in May 1992 for use as staff transport to a Lymington firm. It was photographed in 1982 at the entrance to Victoria Coach Station, London. *(Both: Geoff Coxon)*